HOW TO
MAKE
YOUR
DREAMS
WORK
FOR YOU

HOW TO MAKE YOUR DREAMS WORK FOR YOU

by Dian Dincin Buchman

SCHOLASTIC BOOK SERVICES
New York Toronto London Auckland Sydney Tokyo

ISBN: 0-590-11859-5

Copyright © 1977 by Dian Dincin Buchman. All rights
reserved. Published by Scholastic Book Services, a divi-
sion of Scholastic Inc.

14 13 12 11 10 9 8 7 6 5 4   0 2 3 4 5 6/8

CONTENTS

For Caitlin Dincin Buchman

1

WHAT ARE DREAMS?

Do you remember what happened to you this very morning as you woke up? Perhaps you were lucky enough to stir before the alarm rang and were aware of some fleeting thoughts and images better than any movie you have ever seen. Then the alarm rang and the strange "story" disappeared like smoke.

That was a dream.

What are dreams anyway? Are they just strange episodes during sleep? Are they moving pictures the mind creates?

Dreams are your unconscious mental thoughts during sleep.

"A dream is a description of something

a person is thinking about *without the defenses being up*," says Dr. William Fishbein.

Dreaming is actually a third state of being. The others are waking and sleeping.

Dream thoughts, sometimes with vivid sound, color, and background, chatter continuously through your sleeping mind. Imagine that you are a TV set with access to many different channels; you could then turn on a news show of your own activities. This news show might seem real, like a video-camera taking actual pictures, or be in the style of a super-fast cops and robbers chase. It could be in the form of a spy movie where the bad guys are out to get you, or a love story with a happy ending. How about a science fiction fantasy? Your mind can deliver its episodes dressed in any period of bygone or even future history. Your brain can invent all kinds of stories or show an old fairy tale.

These visual or talking happenings can be tragic or funny, gay or sad, tender or frightening, serene or depressing. They can be ANYTHING.

Maybe you went to bed bone-tired, determined to sleep "hard," or as sleep expert Dr. Julius Segal says, "you may have ducked under the covers to escape reality, but after all you are not a different person when you turn off the light." Actually you take the daytime worries, reactions, and memories to sleep with you.

That is why dream time is a hodgepodge rerun of your waking life.

Isn't the Mind Asleep?

No, your sleeping mind is working every minute, although you aren't aware of it when you are asleep.

There are different brain wave patterns for wakefulness and sleeping. Compare the sleeping brain to a house thermostat set to a low, nighttime, winter month temperature. During this "hold" period your mind selects and classifies all the details of the long day. Oddly, your sleeping mind can even acknowledge people, animals, ideas, and places that you only *partially* noticed during the day, even things you seemingly ignored! In fact your marvelous, super, computerlike mind pigeonholes and analyzes everything that has happened to you.

What Kinds of Things Does the Mind Remember?

Big and little things. It is a giant sorting machine. It takes in all the hurtful things that you thought you ignored, all the small successes; all the chores you forgot; information on who was cheating on that math test; the fact that a girl you like was talking to a guy you hate; the sarcastic remark your gym teacher made to you; the keys you lost; the homework you didn't do. Name it — your mind recorded it some way. But there just isn't time during a busy day to put all these crazy-salad tidbits into place. So the mind does its homework at night when you are sleeping.

This dream mind seems able to compress and expand time, so that the final happenings (you only catch some of them) have nothing to do with time concepts in your waking life.

What Can the Dream Mind Do?

The dream mind is a great artist. It can create paintings. The dream mind can create stories. If you learn to capture your dreams, you might be able to use your inventive dream mind to help you in your creative writing class! (Did you think you couldn't write? Check your dreams for stories!) There even is some literature that has been "discovered" in dreams and then written out afterwards. Are you a fan of the Hobbit series? Well, author Tolkien developed the people, the language, and the place they lived from his dream world. Robert Louis Stevenson also captured his very best stories from his own nightmares and dreams.

Your dream mind can create songs, finish activities you didn't know how to finish, solve simple and difficult problems. Your dream mind can seem to predict your future.

Your dream mind is your honest musing about any and all things that are bothering you or making you anxious and unhappy. Your dream mind is also a calm place of refuge.

One of the most interesting facts on dreams is the capacity of the mind to utilize every bit of the stored past life and experience to crank out its internal "motion pictures."

We *all* dream, and our dreams are reflections of the world in which we exist. We dream every single night we sleep. But why *do* we dream, and why *do* we sleep? What happens in that "first sweet sleep of night"?

2

THE EYES HAVE IT

For centuries people have sought the meaning of sleep.

It was obvious why we needed to be awake. But why did we have to sleep? Was it only a physical body process? In the 20th century, laboratories were created so that determined scientists could stay awake all night and watch how volunteers slept. New and significant facts emerged only when scientists learned to hook up the volunteers to the newest of scientific inventions, those machines that could monitor heartbeat, temperature, brain waves, as well as other vital functions.

In the cause of science the many volunteers permitted the sleepless scientists to awaken them anytime they wished to inquire what was happening during sleep. The scientists wrote down whatever dreams the volunteers could remember in the morning after they awakened. But except for some who were excellent dream recallers, most of the subjects were vague about their dreams. They either said they didn't dream at all, or the dream just disappeared! Most dreams, then, left very little trace.

Then one night, a young graduate student, Eugene Aserinsky, working for the eminent sleep scientist Dr. Nathaniel Kleitman, at the University of Chicago, made a chance discovery. That is why 1953 turned out to be the breakthrough year in sleep research!

This young psychologist had been asked to monitor some brain wave patterns on a sleeping infant. When the brain wave machine showed up some different wave jiggles, he assumed the machine was operating incorrectly. He left the central monitoring room of the sleep laboratory. He was puzzled as he watched the sleeping infant, but the facts he detected eventually changed all of sleep research!

The child's eyes, although closed in deep sleep, seemed to be *darting back and forth under the lids.* It was almost as if the child were watching a tennis match!

When he got back to the control room Aserinsky made note of this brain wave pattern. He also noted that this wave was different from subsequent brain waves when the eyes were more quiet and relaxed during sleep. The next day Dr. Kleitman acted on his assistant's observations and decided to monitor all adult volunteers.

The scientists observed that the adults also had these same *rapid eye movements.* How is it no one had noticed these before? they wondered. Their excitement knew no bounds when over twenty of the sleeping volunteers could actually describe lengthy dreams when awakened during this rapid-eye-movement period of sleep. The scientists decided to call it REM sleep.

After thousands of years of conjecture, the exact moments of dreaming were finally known!

Dream Sleep

Thereafter much of sleep research was divided into REM and Non REM (NREM) sleep. A NREM dream is less vivid and less emotional. The longer, more involved dreams, the ones with conversation and involved with current *problems*, occur during the rapid-eye-movement time.

Stages of Sleep

Just as you nod off, you have fleeting images appearing before your eyes. These are "dreamlets." The rest of your sleep is divided into four stages.

Stage one is light sleep, and you have the first of several REM periods.

Stages two and three are heavier sleep, and during these periods you are *not* having rapid eye movements; thus they are called *N*REM.

The heaviest stage of sleep is stage four: Delta sleep. If you are very tired, you will spend a lot of the nighttime in this stage. But you go from one stage to another back and forth about every ninety minutes.

Therefore the first dream period is short, only a few minutes; but later the dream periods extend to twenty and forty minutes each. The dream time lasts about one fourth of each night — two hours every night.

The Big Dreams

Most of the long involved dreams occur in the last third of the night's sleep . . . toward morning.

That is why the last dream of the night is so often remembered. This is the dream you can capture. This is the dream you can *harvest* each day.

3

WHY DO WE SLEEP?

I bet you could ask a thousand people why they sleep and they would answer, "Because I'm tired." Sleep seems to be restorative. Then, does it exist in man to relieve fatigue? We all know that we go to sleep tired, and most of us get up refreshed.

But that may not be the only answer to why we sleep. Some sleep scientists see sleep as an adaptation of early humans to the cycles of the day and night — in other words, to the light and the dark!

Early man and woman could not function in the darkness, and thus they and other animals are thought to have adapted by slowing down the activity of the body and switching to a sort of "off" cycle.

This was personally demonstrated by Dr. William Dement, a well-known sleep investigator. He drove his car to a remote and dark mountain on a moonless night. He turned off his car lights and walked away from the car in pitch blackness. He writes that he became disoriented and afraid within only a few minutes.

I had the same experience recently when the hall lights and elevator lights were turned off in our apartment house. I entered from the outside where I could see where I was going and decided to ride up in the elevator since I had perishable groceries. The ride to our high floor was eerie, for everything was in total, black-velvet darkness. I thought I would never get there! The worst part was getting out into the scary blackness of what I assumed was my floor. I stumbled around with the packages, found the door, but couldn't get the key into the lock. I began to understand how our cave man and woman ancestors may have felt on moonless nights. They must have welcomed some way to withdraw from the fear they felt!

Was sleep the perfect withdrawal? Maybe sleep was the only way to *adapt to the darkness*.

Recently a new idea on *why* we sleep has been presented. Some researchers think we sleep in order to dream!

These investigators declare that the brain, like a computer, must have some quiet time to reorganize its electrical energy and reprogram and update its different jobs.

One British investigator, Christopher Evans, thinks that dream time is occupied with the processing and sorting out of visual information. He compares the brain to a giant computer that always needs some minor revision.

"Rewriting the program, testing it, running it through, must be done with the computers 'off the line,'" says Dr. Evans. "At that moment they can be reprogrammed, but can't give out information, or take in any new information." Dr. Evans claims this process is very similar to the way the brain works during sleep and dream time.

4

DREAMS ARE THE KEY
TO YOUR MIND

There are two points on which otherwise disagreeing sleep and dream investigators agree.

Dreams, they say, are the key to what is going on in your brain and body. If you understand your dreams, you will understand yourself.

In addition, there are also some researchers who think that dreams are the solution to controlling your external life.

Are Dreams Good or Bad?

There is no such thing as a bad dream! All dreams are good. Even nightmares can be important to you and your life. In nightmares you are processing information that has made or is making you anxious. When you are mature it is helpful to understand, analyze, and overcome anxiety-provoking events and people.

Dreams Are Often about Conflicts

Calvin Hall, the dream scientist, has analyzed thousands of dreams and says that dreams essentially provide us with information about our conflicts. Dreams show us what we are trying to cope with and face up to at a particular time in our life.

According to Hall there are five groups of conflicts. Perhaps you can check and see if your dreams work into any of these categories:

Love and Hate

Life and Death

Freedom and Security

Right and Wrong

Masculine and Feminine

5

WHERE DO DREAMS COME FROM?

Dreams emerge from the events and reactions in everyday life. "No dream can make itself out of nothing. It must be fetched every bit from somewhere." This was said by Anna Freud, daughter of Sigmund Freud. They both helped people overcome emotional troubles. Dr. Freud created the use of dream interpretations to resolve internal burdens.

Whatever the symbols in dreams, the language in each dream represents the internal thoughts, burdens, problems, hopes, and reactions of the dreamer. That is why you can't go to school to learn the language of your dreams, but rather, you must turn inward to learn it.

Sometimes, if you are unable, while awake, to experience or express feelings that are very painful, like anger or fear, they are often released in your dream life. As Dr. Raymond Greenberg of Boston says, "A successful dream removes the pain of a difficult emotion."

That is why it is important to try to record your dreams, as they will help you to understand unexpressed emotions.

What Do Most Young People Dream About?

The largest number of young people remember dreams filled with anxiety, or those related to specific fearful events or deeds. So most young people (and adults) "remove the pain of a difficult emotion" by working it through in dreams.

Up to junior high, nine percent of young people occasionally used the story themes and symbols from fairy tales. A slightly larger group (eleven percent) described dreams involving school, school friends, and school situations. Twenty-two percent dreamed of real people or real things in their lives. A small percentage recalled dreams of hope (jobs they would have, marriages, athletic achievement, success with friends, etc.).

But no matter what the dream content, on close examination the dreams turned out to relate to things that were actually happening in the family, at school, during recreation, or at work.

What Are Some Themes?

The themes are as just mentioned — personal life, school life, hopes for the future, anxiety.

Typical ideas to be found in dreams, ones that keep popping up again and again, are those that deal with *death and dying, chasing and being chased, being found nude in public, taking a test, losing something valuable, missing a train (or plane, or appointment), falling, searching for a room in a house, flying, committing a crime, being punished, being burglarized, losing teeth, climbing.*

The dreams may also be from the Calvin Hall list of *conflicts* — the very things you are working out as you establish your identity. Are your dreams worries about life and death? Or loving and hating? Or getting away from responsibility or getting total freedom? Are they judgments on right and wrong (crime and punishment)? Are they fights over the double side we all have — the masculine and feminine aspects of personality?

Can you think of any other groupings you would like to add?

6

HOW TO LOOK
AT DREAMS

Dreams are fun to unravel. You will find
them as interesting and complicated, as
straightforward yet devious as a good who-
done-it novel. Even disturbing dreams can
bring fresh insights into your life. Your
dreams not only reflect your internal and
honest opinion of the events in your life,
but they are your internal gauge of values.
They can also show you the dark side of
your personality, the things you still have
to deal with and work through before you
will be happy with yourself. The dreams
also show you your resentments and angers
and hostilities, your anxieties as well as
the things you feel guilty about.

Ask Yourself

Check with yourself, once you have written down the details of a dream, for any possible *actual (real) meaning* of the dream story. How does it connect with your life? You frequently find hidden meanings in key scenes, key words, or the *feeling* within the dream (gay, excited, angry, depressed, fearful, etc.).

The "real" meaning in a dream is another expression for literal meaning, a word often used in modern dream interpretation. Investigate these literal meanings first. Don't look for obscure symbols or meanings. The literal meaning is the obvious meaning — the one that first occurs to you. It is one that relates to your daily life or a particular problem occurring at that time.

Taking a Test

Failing an examination is a very frequent dream. But then we all have some anxiety about taking tests. Actually this could indicate many different things. Are you worried about a test, or several tests at school?

But tests come in different forms. Perhaps you feel that you are under fire, under examination by someone, or that someone is testing you in some new situation.

What to Do

What you will do about your findings depends first on your ability to capture the dream and then evaluate it. You will first look for a *literal* meaning, then if necessary, for other possible meanings. You will, if you can, *act on your findings*. Details on *controlling dreams* and *reliving them in daytime or in other dreams* are found in other parts of the book.

Losing Valuable Things

This type of dream may be alerting you to a potential loss in your life through neglect or indifference. Or this might be a questioning of some deeply held values. Perhaps your unconscious is trying to tell you to hold on to something you cherish.

Finding Valuables

This might be a dream of self-worth, of satisfaction with the way you are handling things. It might even be a dream that you *will be* finding something valuable.

22

Crime and Punishment

These are difficult to work out, but they often have something to do with our sense of values, and the conflicts between these values and decisions we have to make in everyday life. They might also have something to do with religious teachings.

Losing Teeth

Have you been neglecting your teeth by any chance? If not, look for other meanings. Teeth represent so many different things. For instance, they can be a turning point (similar to the time you lost your baby teeth). Perhaps you feel like biting someone, or "chewing someone out," or is there an idea you have the urge to "chew on"?

See the way this dream game works?

Whatever the dream, though, it's OK to have it. There are *no* bad dreams!

Flying

It's a great comfort to be floating through the air, and it can offer a lot of release and pleasure. Perhaps it indicates a desire to be forever free of responsibility. It's as if you chose to be a bird in the great game:

"What animal or creature would you choose to be if you were not a person?"

Some well-known psychological interpreters have a lot to say about flying. Freud said it probably related to the childhood pleasure of being carried, swung, or rocked. Alfred Adler, on the other hand, thought such dreams meant you really wished to rise above other people. Carl Jung believed these dreams were a desire to overcome problems.

But first you have to relate these to your everyday life. Do you want to fly higher? Or do you think you have flown too high? (Success can be frightening for some of us.)

But aside from these interpretations, it *can* be fun to take off in flight! Think of the Greek myth of the flying horse Pegasus.

In my dreams I frequently fly away from danger, or give myself the pleasure of soaring through the air to help me find a cheerful, pleasant dream night.

I remember being awakened by a telephone call during a convention visit away from home. Although I had tried to be very comfortable and happy, I had actually been lonely and slightly isolated. The telephone interrupted a terrifying dream which I probably would never have known about.

When I tried to go back to sleep the pursuing and attacking animals wouldn't "go away." I decided that they had to go away, so I mentally changed them into other animals, and gradually they changed again into dolphins. I remember thinking, I wonder if dolphins can fly? Magically, one swam up with reins and I had a dolphin-Pegasus who carried me out of danger!

This is what I mean by having a dreamlet and *reliving the dream* so that the dream can have a happy ending, a successful ending. There is no need to be a victim in life, or in your dreams!

Pursuing, Being Pursued

How does this jibe with your everyday life? Are you chasing after something, or someone, that can never be caught? Are you looking for a rainbow that isn't there? Maybe things are particularly frustrating in your life now.

If you are being pursued you might be living a life with too many pressures *for you*. Think about it, and try to eliminate some of these pressures.

Falling

All of us experience short episodes of quick falling and abrupt awakening. Many people also have longer falls, and some are terrifying.

In the longer and persistent dreams of falling, try to think of a literal connection between your life and the dream. Are you falling down in your work? Do you feel you are falling in the social pecking order at school (power can be the name of the game), experiencing a "fall from grace"?

But falling doesn't have to be a negative experience. Think of the free fall of the parachutists and the fun they have as they glide through the air, and try to change that fall into a positive experience.

Can you die in such a dream fall? I am asked. No, lots of us who share dreams speak of the experience of hitting bottom and recovering. If you feel you are falling and *must* hit the earth and can't change the dream to soaring upward, imagine there is a cushion of some kind for yourself. Feathers? Pine needles? Hundreds of down jackets?

It's your dream — change it any way you want to in the future! How do you do this? To change a dream while you are in the midst of it, you must be aware that you *are dreaming*. Some people sometimes are. Or change the dream the next day in a quick daydream.

Being Nude or Forgetting Lines in Public

Most of us have some experiences, especially in school, when we feel exposed, as if people were looking straight through us to that vulnerable person underneath all those clothes and the "I don't care" attitude. Therefore, the sleeping mind will often capture this lonely and frightened feeling in a dream.

People often have this dream before acting in a play or playing an instrument in public. Even professional actors sometimes have this dream.

Death and Dying

Death, whether it is our own, a person in our family, a friend's, or a stranger's, often emerges in dreams. It is just a part of our life. If it is coming up often, you may be reliving the death of a beloved person. These deaths can be remembered even if they occurred when you were an infant. The writer-poet Thomas de Quincy relived in nightmares the loss of two sisters, one of whom died when he was only eighteen months of age, and the other when he was six years old.

Are you, by any chance, trying to escape something in your life? That doesn't mean you want to stop living, of course, but you may need to get away from something. Or are you literally trying to kill off some unwelcome parts of your own character?

Sometimes these dreams do indicate anger, or a deep feeling of resentment against someone. These are problems you will need to bring out in the open, examine, and clear out.

7

DREAMS OF
PROPHECY

Can we tell the future in our dreams? There is no actual scientific proof that this is possible, although research scientists are working on ESP (extra sensory perception), telepathy (reading someone's mind), and pre-cognition (a sense of the future) in several universities.

Alexander the Great
Young Alexander showed an early genius for military activity, and upon the death of his father, the King of Macedonia, forced the warring city-states of Greece to unite. He then went on to conquer much of the

known world of his day. Like most people in ancient Greece, Alexander was interested in and respectful toward his dreams.

One particular dream of his was retold many times. During an all-night vigil at the bedside of his dying comrade Ptolemy, Alexander fell into an exhausted sleep. In his restless slumber he saw a vision of a serpent, the same one cherished by his mother, Olympias. The serpent carried a plant in its mouth and spoke. "The root of this plant will cure Ptolemy's wound," the serpent predicted.

Immediately upon awakening, Alexander organized a search for the plant. Imagine his excitement when his soldiers discovered the plant growing close to the main tent. When Ptolemy was cured, and other soldiers wounded by the strange arrows were cured, the prophecy of the dream was fulfilled.

Was This Prophecy or Dream Solving?

This dream was certainly in tune with Alexander's known life. His mother, a princess from a primitive hill tribe of Greece, had put great emphasis on the healing plants growing on her native mountains. Her tribe also put unusual stress on the power of snakes. Actually, in ancient times snakes were generally believed to possess magical and curative powers! If you find this strange, check the remnant of this belief by taking a close look at your own doctor's medical symbol, the caduceus. It is a wing-topped staff with *two entwined serpents*!

Much of life in those days was spent outdoors, and Olympias had often showed Alexander her favorite healing plants. Because the subject wasn't of prime importance to the military-directed Alexander, he only paid partial attention to her instruction.

However, when Ptolemy's life was imperiled, Alexander retrieved information from the millions of items stored in his brain. His sleeping mind selected from numerous past memories, including his mother's advice. He was then able to connect the advice to a half-noticed weed at his tent door.

This is a prime example of problem solving with dreams, even though it seems a dream of prophecy. The information was organized through Alexander's mind in the symbolic language of dreams, the "forgotten language," one philosopher has called it. Since Alexander associated snakes with his mother, and snakes were also connected with aspects of healing, a snake emerged as the central figure in his dream drama.

A Famous Roman Dream

This dream concerns Simonides who, while on his way to a sea voyage, discovered a dead body on the road. He stopped to bury it. That night before he was to embark on his ship, he slept in a nearby inn. Here the recently buried dead man came to him in his dream and told him not to go on the ship and said, "If you go, you will die, you will perish in a shipwreck."

Simonides listened to his dream friend and returned home. Later all the persons on that ship died in a shipwreck.

The World's Most Famous Dream Prophecy

The dreams interpreted by Joseph in the Bible are classic. Especially known is Pharaoh's dream of the seven fat cows devoured by the seven lean cows, and the seven fat ears of corn devoured by the seven lean ears of corn.

Joseph's interpretation of each of the fat seven being good harvest years, and each of the lean seven being famine years allowed him to save the country of Egypt by storing grain away during the seven good years.

Was this really prophecy, or problem solving, or both?

8

THOSE HEAVY
DREAMS

Nightmares Can Be OK

Robert Louis Stevenson was a sickly child who had daily nightmares as a youngster. He tried to change these nights of distress, of pursuit and terror and death, into stories to amuse himself and to *control his life*. Later, as he grew older, he actually utilized his active and sensitive dream mind to consciously write the wonderful stories that we have all loved and quaked through during our childhood — *Kidnapped, Treasure Island*, and others. He was so very aware of his dream potential and dreaming ability, that he even invented, and says he used, dream helpers called Brownies.

One night his wife heard him cry out in his sleep and heard him moan so weirdly that she awakened him from his nightmare. He grumpily said, "Why did you do that? I was dreaming a fine bogey tale." This tale turned out to be one of the great chillers of all time: *The Strange Case of Dr. Jekyll and Mr. Hyde.*

Stevenson describes his efforts to work out this chiller-story in his book *Across the Plains.* He says that he had tried for a long time to find a way of telling a story of people's double natures. "[I was] racking my brains for a plot of any sort, and on the second night I dreamed the scene at the window, and the scene afterward split in two; in this Hyde pursued for some crime took the powder and underwent the change in the presence of his pursuers."

Stevenson then said that he wrote the rest of the story during his waking and conscious hours.

It is evident then that Stevenson used his early nightmares to help make him sensitive to his total dream life. He then expanded this dream life into an important part of his creative and working life. Stevenson utilized dream time for creative inspiration, and for the answers to his problems.

What Are Nightmares?

Everyone has had nightmares at one time or other. These are "pictorial reflections of threatening people and events in the dreamers' lives at the time of the dream."

During the rapid-eye-movement part of sleeping, the *body is immobilized*. It cannot move, and that is why it is difficult to cry out in a nightmare, and why it feels even more frightening when, afterwards, we remember it.

A Los Angeles authority on dreams, Dr. William J. Laczek, says the fear factor makes nightmares clearer and easier to remember than pleasant dreams.

Because from an early age we all have an inherent fear of being abandoned, we can have nightmares as early as ten months of age. The peak time may be from two to two-and-a-half years of age. This is the time children feel and act independently, and try to act like the strongest person in the world. But psychologists have discovered that at night very young children, all alone in bed, actually understand the truth of the situation. They aren't the strongest persons in the world. They are quite helpless.

Nightmares are the expression of helplessness.

Very young children are enormously afraid of nightmares, because they haven't had enough life experience to tell what is real from what is unreal. Any pursuing monster, possibly with the real voice of someone known, *seems* real.

Nightmares reflect experiences and feelings that we have buried in our inner minds; it can take months or years to bring them out. These threatening pictures emerge as answers to anxieties in the dreamer's everyday life.

Themes in Many Nightmares

The most basic themes in nightmares are being bitten, devoured, ground up in a big machine, falling, being killed, chased, attacked, or drowning.

Other frequent themes in nightmares in our civilization are trains and automobiles and animals. Each different "invented" object or animal has an entirely different meaning for each dreaming person.

Dr. Laczek has said, "As healthy humans we sometimes try to deny or avoid anxiety or things that upset us. We can suppress these things for a while, but eventually the unconscious will get loaded like a gun and just blow in the form of a nightmare."

A more severe nightmare is one in which a heavy shapeless beast crushes a sleeper's chest as he awakens in terror. This is frequently accompanied by a single terrifying scene of falling, choking, being crushed, or a sense of impending doom.

A less severe nightmare is one in which one is being attacked, pursued, or drowned.

Some dreams are nightmares to the dreamer, though the dream is expressed in seemingly unfrightening symbols.

When Most Nightmares Occur

Nightmares can occur at any age. They are most prevalent when we are anxious, have a sense of inadequacy, or have had a great distress or trauma (like the death of a beloved person in the family). They may also occur if there is a fear of an event that will take place in the future (an operation or even going to the dentist could do it for some people), says Dr. John Mack of Harvard Medical School.

The high period of nightmares is from two to two-and-a-half years (the truly helpless period). There is a better feeling of reality by four years of age, but another increase in nightmares can emerge from ages five to seven, when fifty percent of the dreams are actually unpleasant. This is especially true if there is any anxiety about school.

During ages eight through nine, dreams are easier again, but during the ten-to-thirteen-year period nightmares can again become more frequent. This is because as young people enter puberty there are increases in social pressures, as well as internal physical and emotional ups and downs.

Dream specialists and doctors who work with people troubled by persistent nightmares observe that repeated and continuous nightmares stem from a feeling of severe danger, a threat of danger, powerlessness, a feeling of helplessness, or an overwhelming feeling of anxiety.

Dr. Mack says that unless one outgrows the fears, or seeks to consciously overcome them (we will discuss next how to do just that), the nameless terror, sense of helplessness, and the feeling of violence and persecution in dreams can be preserved throughout a person's life.

It is for this reason that Dr. Mack and

all other dream specialists and people-helpers suggest that each person must find the answers to his or her internal conflicts and struggles.

9

WHAT TO DO ABOUT NIGHTMARES

There is an old saying. Ask for three things: A good friend. A good year. A good dream.

Those people who have persistent and scary nightmares would love to have "good dreams," but they just don't know how. Although there are some older and interesting ideas on dreams (wish fulfillments — Freud; reflection of current motivation and status — Jung; rehearsal or preparation for future activity — Adler), there are some new ideas that not only help to unravel the reason behind a nightmare, but offer a way to prevent it from happening again.

First let us look at some practical aspects. Nightmares can only occur in the total blackness of a room. If you are plagued with persistent nightmares, let in a little light to take the edge off of the blackness! Or at least you could train yourself to put on a light *after* any nightmare occurs. In this way you could immediately reassure yourself that there isn't anyone hiding under the bed, or that some looming thing is trying to capture you. You know this intellectually, of course, but the nightmare seems so REAL!

What you will want to do is *rob this nightmare*, whether it is a persistent one or a loner, *of this sense of realness*.

Many nightmares involve pursuit. Someone or something is pursuing you, the dreamer. A really effective no-nonsense approach to banishing a nightmare when you are having it is to actually say to yourself, "This is a dream. I can change this terrible dream into a better dream. This is my dream, and I can change it!"

To be able to change your dreams while you are dreaming, you must know you are dreaming. To reach the point where this is possible, you have to become a more aware dreamer. Use the methods discussed in the book to do this: Remember your dreams; write them down.

When anyone or anything is pursuing you in a dream you have to turn around — STOP — look at the pursuer — and CHALLENGE it or her or him. I know of one young woman with whom I worked on nightmares who learned to handle them successfully. It was merely a matter of deciding she could control these bad dreams.

I dreamed someone was following me in order to attack me. I was very frightened. *Then it came to me that I was dreaming*, and *I could do something about it in the dream!* So I immediately turned around to this man and screamed: "Why are you following me? GO AWAY!"

The man was frightened by my screaming. He turned to all the other people on the street who gathered around, and he protested that he wasn't trying to attack me at all.

Now I really know I can stop any bad dream from happening! I can do this by changing the dream if I realize I am dreaming, or by redreaming a "good dream" when I wake up from the night-mare.

Sometimes I think about the dream the next day and change it in my mind to a happy or more positive or more successful dream.

Destroy Nightmare Figures

You can not only Stop-Confront-and-Challenge these attackers in your dreams, you can DESTROY THEM, says Clara Stewart Flagg. Mrs. Flagg is a dream seminar leader, and she follows the interesting theories of her late husband, anthropologist Kilton Stewart, who worked with many groups of primitive people. Dr. Stewart discovered that the Senoi tribe in Malaysia learned to destroy all their enemies either in their dreams, or in powerfully directed daydreams where they relived their dreams.

Does that sound strange . . . destroy people and animals in your dreams? Mrs. Flagg says these destructive elements in dreams and nightmares are parts of yourself that actually need destroying so that you can be a more healthy self.

You can do this "banishment" of animals and people in any way you think is pleasant or legitimate. I know I have a terrible time killing off any pursuers, but somehow I don't mind using a "Zap Gun." One time I threw out my hand in a rather queenly gesture and said, "You are just cheese!" And some attacking people melted into an American cheese heap! When I told this to Clara Stewart Flagg she said I should have *eaten* the cheese! She says that's the way to really get rid of all the negative aspects of your personality.

At any rate, you can always say to yourself, "It's only a dream. It's my dream. I can DO ANYTHING I want in my dream!"

Then go ahead and change the dream around. Make it a good dream. Make the pursuers afraid of you. Then tell them to come to you to shake hands. Use the Senoi technique. *Make every dream enemy a dream friend.* The Senois went even further in this — they made every new dream friend give them a gift of some sort in their dream.

Change the Nightmare into a "Good"-mare

Use a wand, use a rod, use a zap gun, use an arrow, a sling, a rock, or just your voice. Use any technique that you like, as long as you are the winner in the dreams. It is your dream world, you know.

If you dream of drowning, have someone save you.

If you dream of huge monsters, have them fall into a pit way before they can get to you, and bury them once and for all. That monster will never come to haunt you again!

Nightmares never return to disturb you once you challenge them and tell them not to bother you again!

Sounds very simple, doesn't it? What you have to do is concentrate, become a more aware dreamer, Stop-Confront-Challenge-and-Destroy.

If you dream a persistent nightmare of a house without windows or doors, redream it and create beautiful windows that open up onto the sea or a garden with sunshine and greenery for your view. (And then try to examine why you feel so boxed in in your daily life.)

If there is a machine coming after you night after night, use your electrical zapper and stop all the machinery from ever working again.

Always have yourself *rescued* in a bad dream! Always have yourself *helped* in

your bad dream. ALWAYS HAVE YOUR-
SELF THE FINAL WINNER in a nightmare.

Do this by changing the dream as you
are dreaming, or redream the dream after
you awaken, or during a quiet daydream
period the next day.

Reliving the Dream

Talking about your dream the next day
is excellent anti-nightmare insurance. By
sharing it with friends or family you can
actually "see" and "hear" all the details of
a dream that has bothered you. Once you
have voiced the awful details out loud they
won't have quite the same force again. All
the better if you have acquired (or even
attempted) the Stop-Confront-Challenge-
Destroy technique. That will be the last
time you will have to endure that same bad
experience.

According to Ann Faraday, one of the
most astute dream observers, you should
also learn to give the attacker a "voice."
She says that you should ask the attacker
what it wants of you. Ms. Faraday says
this strips the attacker, whether it is a
person or an animal, of the fearful energy
that it can have in the dream. This also

gives you the experience of finding out what is really bothering you, since these nightmares are triggered by certain events and problems.

Bring Back the Monster

One doctor who worked with children had this technique to help them get rid of persistent and threatening monsters.

He would have the child draw the monster. He then sat the child on his lap, and would say, "Close your eyes, and see the monster.

"Is the monster there?" he would ask.

"Yes," the child would reply.

"MONSTER, GO AWAY," the doctor would shout. "Monster, we don't want you here ANYMORE."

He would tell the child to open his or her eyes. Then they would repeat the same situation over again. The child would close his eyes and envision the monster. Again the doctor would tell the monster to go away and not bother the little child again.

Fairly soon, the child would open his or her eyes right after seeing the monster and also shout, "GO AWAY. I DON'T WANT YOU ANYMORE!!!!"

The monster would then disappear from that child's life.

You can do the same thing to any annoying persons or things in your dreams.

10

WHAT'S A NIGHT TERROR?

There are two forms of problem dreams, say physicans and dream specialists. One is called the nightmare. The other is called a night terror.

In a nightmare, the troubles in the dream often awaken you, and more often than not, nightmares can be remembered. But in a night terror, the person who dreams the terrifying fantasy is hard to arouse, almost never wakes up during the episode, and usually remembers nothing of the bad dream at all.

Night-terror victims will often sit up in bed and breathe and perspire heavily while still asleep. The disturbance can continue for a few minutes to a half an hour, but after that everything in the body seems to relax and the dreamer goes back to a quieter sleep.

The doctors report that most young people grow out of·these terrors!

Overcoming a Night Terror or Nightmare

Take a relaxing warm bath. Always remember to close your pores with cool water. Vigorously rub your body with a heavy bath towel. Arrange to have a cup of hot sleep-producing herb teas. Chamomile and linden plus honey are two favorites. (See the sleep chapter in *How to Feel Good and Look Great* — Scholastic.)

Have an anticipation of a good night's sleep free of any disturbance.

Right before going to sleep say out loud when you are alone, or to yourself if you are sleeping in a room with lots of sisters or brothers, "Dreams, why are you frightening me? Dreams, I don't want to be frightened anymore. Dreams I want to sleep more peacefully."

This kind of question, and these kinds of statements to your dream mind are very successful anti-nightmare, and anti-terror techniques.

11

HOW TO FIND
YOUR ANSWERS

Did you know that you could use your
sleep time to help you work on and solve
problems that are bothering you? In fact,
answers to knotty problems have occurred
to all kinds of people in their dreams! Some
of the world's leading scientists, athletes,
scholars, writers, painters, and musicians
have even unraveled technical questions
during their dream time.

The world-famous golfer Jack Nicklaus
was in a bad slump one year, and since
golf is not just a pastime but a profession
with him, he thought about the reason for
his slump day and night. Then one morn-

ing he awakened from a vivid dream in which he had hit all of the golf balls with uncanny accuracy. Was it just a wish on his part, he speculated, or had he actually done something differently in this dream? Nicklaus lay quietly reviewing what it was he had done. As if he were watching a movie of a game, he reviewed each move he had made. There it was! He was using an entirely new stance and a new grip.

Nicklaus concentrated on remembering these new postures and then rushed out to the golf course to try them out. In the quiet time of sleep his mind had *worked out* the perplexing questions of style. After that he went on to play top championship golf.

The discoverer of the unique properties of Vitamin C, Nobel Prize-winner Albert Szent-Gyorgyi, is a great believer in "sleeping on his problems." "I often wake up with answers to questions that have been puzzling me," he says.

The late pianist Gina Bachauer has said the very same thing about her music:

Musical problems are on my mind when I wake up. I suppose I go to sleep with them and think about them subconsciously, for sometimes I wake up in the middle of the night, and discover I am thinking and playing a fugue!

Sometimes when I've had a difficult technical problem with a piece of music, I can get up in the morning and go to the piano and find that I have solved it.

The very foundation of modern chemistry, the solution to the elusive benzene structure, was a problem that had eluded scientists. Fredrich A. Kekulé, a German chemist, had been working on this problem for a long time. One night in 1865 he fell asleep. Let him describe what happened that night:

Again the atoms were juggling before my eyes. My mind's eye sharpened by repeated sights of a similar kind could now distinguish larger structures of different forms and in long chains, many of them close together; everything was moving in a snakelike and twisting manner. Suddenly, what was this?

One of the snakes got hold of its own tail, and the whole structure was mockingly twisting in front of my eyes. As if struck by lightning, I awoke . . .

The snake holding its own tail provided Kekulé with the insight to the closed carbon ring, and the six snakes in the dream helped him to envision the hexagon shape of the benzene ring. This proved to be "the most brilliant prediction to be found in the whole range of organic chemistry."

Kekulé had so much faith in the power of the dreaming mind to find answers that he told a scientific convention meeting honoring him, "Let us learn to dream, gentlemen, and then we may perhaps learn the truth."

The Nobel Prize-winner Otto Loewi has said that his prize was based on information that had "come to him" while he was dreaming. These insights proved to be the foundation of his theory of chemical transmission of nerve impulses.

Many scholars who have puzzled during the day over intricate jigsaw puzzles of information have sometimes "discovered" the total answer during their dream time. One of the most famous of these experiences occurred to the classic scholar Professor Herman V. Hilprecht of the University of Pennsylvania. After working past midnight deciphering an ancient fragment of a Babylonian ring, he had a vivid dream in which an ancient priest unraveled the inscription and told him it was not a ring, but one of two *ear*rings.

Since Hilprecht was only working from drawings, he decided to go to Constantinople to find the original agate fragment. There he discovered that there were indeed two different earring fragments stored in separate cases. When placed together, the inscription worked out as his dream priest had advised!

Did his mind just piece together the puzzle and reveal the solution in the symbolic language through the priest, or was this a dream of the future? All we know is that everyone can try to work out problems in their dreams, and more often than not, the answers do come.

Do You Like to Solve Puzzles?

What does OTTFF mean?

This forms the beginning of an infinite sequence. Find a simple rule for determining any or all successive letters.

A scientist found the above puzzle in a book. That night he had this dream solution:

I saw myself in an art gallery, and I began to count the paintings. 1-2-3 ... But as I came to the sixth and seventh paint-nigs, I saw they had been ripped from the frames. I stared hard at the paintings thinking that the mystery was about to be solved. Suddenly I realized the sixth and seventh spaces were the solutions to the problem.

The answer is *One, Two, Three, Four, Five*
          O   T   T   F   F

12

FAMOUS DREAM ANSWERS

Dream experimenters and mind researchers have discovered there are several ways to solve problems in dreams. The most important ingredient in dream solutions is awareness of the problem and desire to find the answer.

One of the simplest solutions is to quietly talk to yourself just before going to bed. Say to yourself and your dream mind, "Dream, I need an answer to a problem. Dream, I would like to find the answer in my dream. This is the problem." (You state the problem in one or two sentences. If you find that the problem seems complicated to say, take a pencil and paper and *write* it out clearly.)

The 72-Hour Solution

One of the remarkable and effective techniques taught for hundreds of dollars at the Silva Mind Control Sessions is the water-glass solution finder. As you go to bed take a glass of water with you, and put it on the table next to your bed.

State out loud, or write down in one or two clear sentences, one problem to which you wish you had an answer. It can be anything from: Why don't I get along with my — brother — sister — mother — father — teacher — or friend? to Why doesn't____ like me anymore? How can I do better in school? What should I do to be a better athlete? How can I be more popular and keep my own standards? Is there any way I can be happier in my life? Why can't I stop smoking? Shall I go to college? What careers would I enjoy as an adult?

These are only examples, of course. You will make up your own statements that refer to anything that bothers or puzzles you in your daily life. You can state any problem that you have on your mind.

After stating the problem as concisely as

possible, drink one half of the water in the glass.

Go to sleep, and make up your mind to sleep soundly.

When you wake up the next morning, drink the other half of the water in the glass.

In seventy-two hours you may have the answer to your question. It may not hit you over the head — like, aha, there it is — but during the course of these hours after you have stated your problem you may discover you have made some judgments, and you may have one or several possible answers that will work out well for you. You may just have a new sense of relief about an anxiety that has been troubling you.

After you have worked through one problem successfully, you can try out another important question several days later, and so on. Your sleeping-but-working mind, free of all distractions, guilt, and burdens of your everyday life, will, like the marvelous computer-type machine that it is, find out, sort out, unravel, and decipher the things you have on your mind!

Remember, though, only one question at a time until you can get your complicated brain working.

13

DAYDREAMING

A daydream is a reverie away from the activities in which you are then involved. If this occurs during the school hours, it could be for several reasons: a safety valve to escape from troubles; lack of air in the room; lack of interest in the subject; lack of ability to concentrate; lack of desire to concentrate. It could also be from lack of brain food — protein.

If you eat a good solid breakfast with some protein, or hot oatmeal (this releases sugar very slowly and keeps away hunger pangs), you should have less trouble concentrating. It also helps if you open the window for some fresh air, or if you can dash out the door for fresh air between classes. In winter, the steam heat and the excessively heated classrooms create a feeling of additional fatigue.

But daydreams do not have a negative connotation to me at all. I like daydreams. I use daydreams to enhance my life and help me to live pleasantly and calmly.

Dr. Jerome Singer of Yale University daydreams when he goes to the dentist. He uses these dreams to divert the pain and calm his mind.

Dr. Jean Mundy of Long Island University also uses daydreams and/or alpha waves when she goes to the dentist. She never has to take a novacain shot for the pain. Dr. Mundy taught herself this technique with the use of a simple bio-feedback machine. She learned how to identify her alpha waves (the same brain waves that you have as you are falling asleep), found a daydream that can bring on the brain waves, and "retrieves" the daydream when she wants to overcome pain. Incidentally, the same idea can be used to overcome anxiety, fear, or depression. Such brain wave training, a sort of controlled daydreaming, is now used for migraine headaches, hypertension, and a host of other health problems. This kind of training can only be learned with the help of an expert in biofeedback.

Dr. Singer has worked with thousands of people in his practice and has decided that the daydream should be *encouraged*. He encourages people to take travel daydreams, to cruise away to some marvelous foreign land, and quickly return (in their minds, of course).

The reason Dr. Singer encourages people to daydream is that the daydream, like the night dream, can provide answers to previously unsolvable problems. These dreams can help you to spot key connections of riddles we carry in our minds.

He suggests you let your eyes wander to the left (this provides better visual imagery), to put on soft and lilting music, or even the music of the country you want to "travel to." He suggests that poor visualizers obtain some pictures of that country, or a book from the country as a base for the traveling.

It is obviously important to do this armchair traveling or daydreaming when you are in a safe environment. Don't do it when you are in an athletic game, or driving, or doing your chores, or in a classroom, or in a situation to which you should be giving your full attention.

Dr. Singer has found that all of us have the ability to daydream or to produce some imaginative thought unrelated to the tasks that confront us. He has also determined that people who *never* daydream may need more outside stimulation. That means that they might be more susceptible to alcohol and drug abuse than people who do daydream on occasion.

Daydreaming then not only can provide relaxing diversion from difficult days, but can provide interesting and important new experiences.

However, excessive daydreaming, daydreaming instead of living, is *not* a good thing. If you feel your life is *only* satisfying when you are daydreaming, something is wrong!

14

HOW TO REMEMBER YOUR DREAMS

There is a theory that dreams are made to disappear from our minds so that the mind will not confuse the dream (remember, all kinds of strange and beautiful and fantasy things happen in dreams) *with real memory* of the things, places, and people that we have had contact with.

Should You Remember Your Dreams?

You may be in that half of the population that hardly ever recalls the substances of dreams. You may only remember a small part of the very last dream of the night, the one in the morning before you wake up.

Or you may think you never remember dreams.

Should you?

Ultimately, that will be your own choice.

But since dreams are one of the very best insights into your own hidden thoughts, it is useful to know your dreams. Understanding and knowing your dreams can help you to cope with your worries, guilts, fears, and hopes.

Dreams, then, can help you to control your life.

How to remember your dreams: If you haven't a natural aptitude, you can develop lots of ways of "harvesting" the rich life of your dreams.

The first thing you have to do is really want to know more about your dream life. Talk to others about their dream lives too. It's great to share these dream experiences and to help each other learn. But don't lay any heavy interpretations on someone else's dreams!

Each dream language is personal. If someone does share his or her dreams with you, DON'T REPEAT THEM TO ANYONE ELSE. That would be mean and ungenerous.

Set the Stage for Capturing Dreams

Have a notebook ready by your bedside. Have a pencil or a pen placed in a position so that you can easily find it in the dark, even with your eyes closed.

If you sleep in a room with other people, try to buy a night-writer pen with a small flashlight in it. Many stationery stores carry such pens.

Tell yourself before you go to bed that you want to remember your dreams.

When you stir in the morning, or during the night, lay there very quietly (motion sometimes seems to make the dreams disappear). Try and recall what you were dreaming about. Slowly adjust your body in the bed with very little movement. Try to remember what you were thinking about.

Sometimes people don't realize they were dreaming, because they assume it was "thinking." Either way the mind has been working away, finding answers and making picture-events of things that happened in your life. Try to capture the essence of the thoughts.

Give the thinking a title. This is a little like the title of a book or a movie. Just pick out one or two facts that seem to "fit" the dream. Even one word will do. That will also help you to remember it later.

Work backwards, and try to "see" where you were in that dream.

Try to remember what you were doing, or what was happening.

What colors were in that dream?

What are the *feelings in the dream?*

This is very important. Do you feel sad, angry, happy, gay, excited, depressed, afraid?

You might want to keep in mind the statement of the great German poet Goethe. "Human nature possesses wonderful powers, and it has something in readiness for us when we least hope for it. There are times when I have fallen asleep in tears, but in my dreams the most charming forms have come to console me, and cheer me, and I have risen the next morning fresh and joyful."

Then don't go back to sleep for those beloved next "forty winks," even if you long for another long snooze. This is the time to slowly reach for your dream journal or log.

15

DREAM JOURNAL

A dream journal is your own private and secret log. It can consist of one or two, or even three or four different parts.

The log itself consists of any random and remembered thoughts about the dream as well as your first and second reaction to the dream. This is the log you will keep to help you remember the full content of your week, your month, your year. Naturally you will know more about yourself if you happen to write in the log every day, but that might not be possible or convenient. Write in this log as often as you can, and as often as you wish. Do not feel compelled to keep this journal, but rather do it as a private and personal adventure in tracking your mind and its internal thoughts.

The log can also include drawings of any of the scenes, people, paintings, buildings, objects, even monsters that have come to you in your dream world.

After you have put your thoughts down when half-awake, you might want to reconstruct your dream world into a more formal sequential log. For this reason a possible dream log is shown on pages 74–75. You do not have to follow these ideas, but might like to invent and create your own personal code. However, checking off these details time and again will stimulate your dream recall and help you to sharpen your dream memory.

The *date* is important so you can later check the relation between dreams and your everyday life. If you decide you would like to make pre-dream jottings in your journal (description is at the end of this chapter), you will inevitably see the relationship of your life and your dreams. This will also give you a record of how often you have dreamed.

The number should be listed in case you

can record more than one dream in a night. It is good to mention and record even fragments and wispy parts of a dream. This will help to train your mind to capture the dreams before they totally disappear. Remember, *anticipation* of dreaming and remembering the dreams helps to recall all kinds of dreams.

It is very helpful to give the dream a *title* — one or two words or a sentence that gives the essence of the whole dream. This will also help you to remember the details in the dream as you can work backwards around the phrase.

The *place* of the dream; the *color*; the *sounds* in the dream (you can define them or just say strong or soft, for instance); the *images (visual)*, whether weak or strong, memorable, real, or imaginative: all are elements that you should try to notice and record. As you get more experienced and interested in dreaming you will notice more and more of these important details.

It sometimes helps you to notice whether you are an *active participant* or a *passive onlooker* in a dream. This might be significant in terms of the way you feel about yourself, or the problems you are working on in your dream mind.

For example, it is generally understood that riding in a car, train, or plane can focus on important aspects of your life. Now, whether or not you are doing the driving or are a passive passenger *is* very significant. It's your dream, it's your life. Shouldn't you be doing your own driving?

I discussed this with a young woman who shared many of her dreams with me. She was always the passenger, and I pointed this out. "But I don't know how to drive," she said. "It doesn't matter," I retorted. "You say you want to be in charge of your life more. You say you want to learn to be independent. In that case you have to learn to drive the car, and *you* have to drive it!"

Several weeks later she called me in glee. "I drove the car in my dreams last night! And lots of other things seem to be falling in place in school and with friends too!"

But generally speaking there is no judgment that should be made by you about the details in the dream. There is nothing to be guilty about in reviewing any dream. That is what is happening. It is just for your appraisal and evaluation.

In the *description* of your dream you will note all kinds of details: *words, dates, numbers, names, people, faces, feelings.* Next to it, you will write down your first reaction, even questions you are asking yourself as you are writing the description and remembering the dream. Try to sort out and relate any facts that are connected with events of the day or events of the week. These can be external things from exams to lateness, to troubles, to hopes and fears, to struggles in your friendships, to reactions to teachers or family.

Don't forget to underline the important words, the key ideas. And, of course, don't miss the fun of discovering the puns in your dreams, or the crossover words, or the words that might indicate your deep-down, hidden feelings.

"I saw a chicken all trussed up, ready for the oven. Then the butcher wrapped up a lot of other packages." The key words here probably are trussed and wrapped. Is it that the person feels "under wraps," "all trussed up," or is it a pun on the word trust? Are these ideas connected? That is the way your mind will work as you analyze the visual elements and the words of your dream.

MY DREAM LOG

Date			
Dream Number			
Remember: Whole, Part, None			
Dream Title			
Feeling in Dream			
Brief Description of Dream			
Place			
Color			
Sound			
Visual Images			
Voices			
Active or Passive			
How Dream Relates to My Life			

Before-Sleep Dream Diary

If you are interested in dream work, or if you want to recall your dreams better than you have been doing, you might consider doing some diary writing about thirty minutes before going to bed.

You can plan to do this about one night a week, and it will surely help you to relax and to understand a little more about yourself. Many great statesmen, writers, journalists, and many good solid citizens of the world have kept diaries of their reactions, observations, and memories of the day. But this diary isn't like an ordinary diary with every small moment recorded.

This diary writing will be on one quiet night of the week. Have your notebook and pen ready on your bed. Take a quiet bath (better for relaxation than a shower, by the way), and pop into bed.

In the notebook you will write about *any* of the problems that are bothering you. Do this for about twenty-five minutes or so. The last five minutes of this thirty-minute diary session can be summary. Try to think of a one-line condensed sentence that summarizes *one* problem you want answered. If you have more than one, write it down, if you like, to use on another night.

16

DREAM WORD PUZZLES

Do you like playing word games? Your mind does. In your dreams your mind will often use words in odd ways and you have to ponder the double meanings, extract the puns within the dreams, and look for reverse meanings in phrases and words.

In talking with scores of young people about dreams, we discovered interesting hidden word clues to essential feelings in dreams. They were not always obvious, of course, but after examining the literal meaning of key words, the second choice of dream examination was detective work on these same words.

A young woman had several different dreams of acting on the stage. Upon examination of her life at the time, she came to the conclusion it meant making decisions, *acting on* family problems. A college-bound friend dreamed of walls with light switches. The hidden meaning was his feeling that he should *switch* his application from a larger to a smaller college. I dreamed of a reclining lion — a double pun for *lying down* on a job I had to do.

A dream in which a young man used a carpenter's level actually referred to his bitter feeling that his friends were not *"on the level"* with him. Being surrounded by gnats in a camping trip pointed out to another young person a resentful feeling of *"being bugged"* by his family.

A landslide suggested the *"washout"* quality of a planned summer project. Mending the skirt of a friend pointed out the deep feeling about a chum who had been in an automobile accident (*that her leg would mend*). A wall filled with dusty pink glasses signaled an intuition that a young person was looking at everything with *rose-colored glasses*. Missing the bull's-eye on a dart board indicated the gut feeling of *"missing the mark"* in social life.

Occasionally, elusive dreams can be interpreted when key words are reversed or extracted. A baseball dream symbolized the feelings of the dreamer that something in his life was underhanded or *base*. Standing under a bridge archway was soon interpreted as needing *understanding*.

Clara Stewart Flagg in her dream seminars loves to point out the appropriateness of dream puns. I have heard her point out that the dream in a bar might mean the feeling of being *barred* from doing what one likes; that walking on a city block in a dream might mean a gut feeling of being *blocked off* in a part of one's life.

The mind can refer to slang terms, too, as in one dream in which a young girl reported wearing huge eyeglasses. She later decided they signified "cheaters," a term for glasses, since this referred to her feeling about her boyfriend.

Seeing a "bureau" on her upper torso led to a double pun for one young women. "I've got to get something off my chest," she declared, after thinking hard about the dream and her feelings about the day preceding the dream.

I can recall two dreams recently where the key words were funny twists. In one dream I saw a little red worm with green eyes come out of a canteloupe. When I awakened, the first thing I could think of was why did I dream of a tapeworm? This gave me my clue. In an indirect, symbolic way I was dreaming about *red tape*. This referred to a difficult project I was involved in.

In a second dream I saw a container of well water being delivered to my daughter Cait. When I mentioned it the next morning, she caught the meaning before I did — " 'Well' water, Mom. I've been sick, and you want me to be *well*."

When such a remark hits a nerve and it feels *true*, you know it's the right interpretation.

That's why I love to share dreams with family and friends, and that's why finding the hidden symbolic message in a dream feels as good as solving a difficult puzzle.

17

DREAM YOUR WAY TO SUCCESS

In a remote corner of Malaysia there is a primitive tribe, the Senoi. They were first discovered by anthropologist Patrick Noone, and then investigated by still another anthropologist, Kilton Stewart.

The Senoi live in long houses and have strong community and family ties. When a Senoi youngster wakes up, the first thing his parents ask are questions about his or her dreams the night before. This sharing of the dreams sharpens interest in recall. The young people tell all their fantasies, they sing the songs they heard in their dreams, they draw the pictures they saw in their dreams, and they tell the stories they imagined in their dreams. In this way all kinds of nasty, fearful, horrible, good, kind, and helpful images emerge.

But the Senoi not only *listen* carefully to each person's daily dream, they actually plan their lives to fulfill the purpose of the last night's dream, or to overcome the problem found in the dream during the night.

The astonishing thing is that these primitive people have learned an effective way of dealing with dreams. Every child learns to redream bad dreams until they are happy dreams. In Senoi life, the only successful dream is one in which the dreamer is a victor.

All bad, difficult, scary things are worked out, either in the dream or the redream. The Senoi instruct their dream mind as to the outcome of the next dream — and the dream mind responds!

In Senoi dreams, mean people, bad, hurtful objects, fierce animals or monsters are changed into friends.

In the Senoi tribe, each dream friend must offer a dreamer a gift in the dream or redream. This is not an ordinary gift as you and I know it. It is something precious, like a song, or a drawing, or a flower, a plant, a fresh fish, or some special knowledge.

The explorers and scientists who lived with these people say that the Senoi are the nicest, kindest, least selfish, and most generous people they have ever known. They say there is no crime, no murder among these people. The anthropologists say this is so because the Senoi work out their problems, angers, and aggressions in their dream world.

18

DREAM QUESTIONS

Q: I would like to know if it is normal to dream?

A: Oh, absolutely. WE MUST DREAM. We have four to six deep-sleep periods during the night that are each about twenty minutes in length. (The first one is shorter, and the last one may be the longest.) These "Delta" wave dreams are about ninety minutes apart.

During the REM (rapid eye movement) stage of sleep the brain is producing a certain kind of brain wave. Scientists think that during this sleep the brain retrieves all kinds of memories from early childhood on in order to form dream sleep. The things, objects, people, and visions that we retrieve are thought to be triggered by an event during the day.

Interestingly, scientists have come to the conclusion that the amount we remember in daily life is related to the kind of dreaming and the amount of dreaming we had the night before.

So you see, it is normal to dream. If you believe you had a "dreamless sleep," this is an illusion of memory.

Q: Is dreaming good for you? Why or why not?

A: Dreaming is good for you. It is your various selves, as well as the alienated parts of your life, emerging. It is the "story" of the things you are avoiding in your daily and probably pressured life.

If you can capture your dream or dreams in a notebook-journal you will have a record of the things you should be working out and facing up to, as you try to create a mature identity for yourself.

Dr. Ramon Greenberg of the Boston Veterans Administration Hospital says, "Dreams allow us to draw on our past experiences so we can change our present."

Q: I have a hard time falling asleep every night. What can I do?

A: This is a problem that many people have. But sleep is a state you have to anticipate. You must want to sleep, and you have to know how to give in to sleep. You can prepare for sleep just as you prepare to go to school in the morning.

Try warm baths, always ending with cooler and cooler water, and if you can, with cold water on your ankles. Drink herb teas, such as chamomile, peppermint, or linden. You can try that age-old folk remedy, warm milk and honey. It's very relaxing.

Q: What is happening when you wake up in the night and you believe you weren't dreaming anything?

A: Dreams, like smoke, disappear quickly. Your "thoughts" at the time you awakened were probably a part of a dream. Many of us decide we are thinking, and don't associate these thoughts with activities within a dream.

Without moving about in the bed, try to reconstruct the feelings, places, and people in your mind at that time and the total picture of your dream comments may come back to you.

Q: How come on some nights you dream and other nights you don't?

A: You don't remember, but you *have* dreamed!

Scientists, including Dr. Rosalind Cartwright of the University of Illinois, say that mental activity during sleep is on an equal footing with mental activity during the day. "Mental activity is continuous. It changes in character, but it's always with us. There is no time off for good behavior, not even during sleep." All this means, of course, that the nighttime mental activity, the "visualizations without any defenses," are the activities we call dreams.

The answer then is to train yourself to recall these dreams.

This can only come about with practice. The well-known pianist and composer Paderewski once said, "If I go one day without practicing then I can tell the difference. If I go two days without touching the piano then my friends notice the difference as well. After three days my audience knows the difference."

Practice in anything keeps you in top form.

Q: What is the best way to remember dreams?

A: Write them down immediately after quietly reconstructing all remembered details. Otherwise, in five minutes only fragments are left of the dream. Most dreams disappear after ten minutes if not "harvested."

I use a hardback composition book, or a medium-sized spiral notebook. I don't use looseleaf pages or separate pages, as these tend to disappear.

I always keep a flashlight pen by my bedside table so as not to disturb my husband, although we share the dream in the morning. I try to recall all elements that I have listed in my dream log chart, but if I don't, I don't worry. Each dream remembered is its own reward and allows me the pleasure of exploring the connection to my everyday life.

Q: How come dreams get worse and worse while you are growing up?

A: This adolescent stage of your life may be the most difficult one of all. All kinds of new hormones are developing in your body at the same time that complicated school, social, boy-girl relationships also emerge. It is the time of your life when your family and teachers expect more things from you, and there are increasing responsibilities. Many of these problems will sort themselves out one way or another. As you progressively learn to control different aspects of your life, when you accomplish more that you can be happy about, and have successes in the projects you are engaged in, your dreams will reflect your new ability to cope with life.

Q: If you dream of death, do you die?

A: No. Almost everyone dreams of death or dying at one time or another. Death is sometimes a part of some nightmares too.

It may mean that you are angry at someone in your family or someone in school. Like the Queen in *Alice in Wonderland*, you are shouting, "Off with her [or his] head!"

If the dream is about the death of someone you know, you might want to check into your feelings about this person at that time. Telling your family or friends or teachers that you are hurt by something can often turn a festering situation into a more neutral or relaxed situation.

At any rate, although you may dream of others dying, and you may dream of yourself dying, it is the *language* of the dream that is important. Ask yourself what has happened to you in the last few days or months that has caused you to dream of death, and how does it connect in a real or indirect way to your daily life.

When you analyze your dreams in relation to everyday existence — the hurts, the joys, the problems, the interactions between you and other people — they will become easier to understand.

Some dream seminar leaders insist that every dream image is a part of the dreamer's life — meaning *your* life. So whatever you dream is a part of you. You are not causing someone's death if you dream of his or her death in a dream, and it doesn't mean that you will be dying right then and there either! However, it could mean that some destructive *parts of you* are being allowed to die. So also check out if you are trying to rid yourself of some unwanted characteristic, and your dream mind is commenting on it.

Q: What are most dreams about? I say that most people's dreams are about their country [where they live], or something that happened that day. Am I right?

A: Right! Dreams are about life and happenings of that day, the past day, or things that remind you of past events.

Q: Why is it that most times when you wake up you can't remember what you dreamed, but some dreams are crystal clear?

A: No one knows the reason this happens. But, somehow, important dreams often seem clear and sometimes occur again and again as you work through problems that you need to solve in your life. But you can train yourself to make *more* dreams a part of your life. See the chapter on recall.

Q: Do the things you do during the day have anything to do with what you dream? Do your dreams come from events that happened in the past?

A: The dream world is a retrieval system that usually relates to the events in one's life. But since everything you have EVER seen — especially since you were two years old and after — in person, on TV, in the movies, or *heard*, or *read* about, is available for your computerlike brain, you can dream about it.

In addition, recent research has indicated that your dream time during REM sleep "fixes" memory in the mind.

Q: Why do we have good dreams some nights and bad dreams other nights?

A: Not every good day means good dreams, or every bad day, bad dreams. But dreams follow life, and each day we live, each activity we are involved in, and each interaction with another person is different. The dreams are your sorting out of problems and are inner comments to the many things that happen to you during your day. Your dreams are evaluating your feelings and reactions of the day (and days before).

If you are having a particularly hard time with bad dreams, you can ask your dreams to advise you as to the reason. Also ask your dreams for ways of coping better with these problems.

Q: I am so glad to hear about this dreaming book, because I dream about this dead relative all the time. What should I do not to dream about this person?

A: Frequently there are unresolved issues between the mourner and the person who has died. After all, it is very easy to remember the things we should have said and the kindly things we might have done for this person before he or she died.

Undoubtedly, it is time to say good-bye. This is very hard to do when you are grieving for a relative or a dear friend. This is the good advice I have heard from many experts who work with people who are in a mourning state for a long time. They suggest that you make up your mind to have a good-bye service. You will be interested in learning that often the person who is being mourned for such a long time in dreams occasionally appears in these dreams to ask the mourner *to stop grieving*. Sometimes there is even a request to the mourner to go on with the business of living!

Q: How come a friend you really like gets hurt in a dream?

A: You can like someone very much but still feel angry at this person about a particular interaction between you. Or you can have hostile feelings to someone that you are hiding from yourself.

However, it is also possible that your friend is a stand-in for you and some trouble or trauma that you are working out in your dream mind. Dreams are "messages from the interior," says Dr. Chester Pearlman of the Boston Veterans Administration Hospital. Once you "capture" the dream it's up to you to discover the message you should be heeding.

Q: I am a boy of 13. About a year ago a friend of my parents told me that all dreams were in black and white, and they were all abstract. But my sister, my brothers, and I, and many of our friends dream in color! Are dreams abstract, and are they in color or in black and white?

A: Dreams *are* in color, but each person remembers dreams differently. The colors seem to run true to real life, as found in nature. However, even good recallers don't always remember the colors in their dreams. To help jog the memory on this I added COLOR to the dream log list, so that dreamers could remember to check it off whenever they could.

Being on the alert for certain things in dreams, such as color, sound, visual elements, place, time, numbers, dates, names, and words, can help you to sharpen your dream recall.

As for abstract versus concrete — a certain percentage of young people as well as adults dream about real-looking things, and real-life situations. Dreams are not always disguised in that unique "hidden" language of dream symbols.

So in a way your parents' friend is right. His dream world is black and white, and consists, as he recalls it, of symbols. Your dreams are remembered with vivid color, and at this stage of your life seem to be totally realistic.

Each person in the world has an entirely unique (and yet somewhat similar) dream language and code. Learning to understand this language and code can go a long way to help you to understand yourself, your goals, your fears, your wishes — all the things that make you tick!

Q: If I were to hit the ground during my dream would I have died?

A: No. The next time you have a dream like this, try changing the fall into a free-fall parachute jump for fun, or try changing the direction of the fall by flying or soaring.

Q: Why do most dreams show violent death? In most of my dreams death seems to be a frequent happening. Sometimes I'm even the victim!

A: Daily dreams of death are not necessary but obviously indicate a sense of doom about your daily life and problems. Taking up such matters with a sympathetic professional will probably help you to understand the conflicts, forces, and events in your life that influence your thinking.

I hope you will become more aware of the factors which are now bothering you, and through additional thinking, journal evaluation, *sharing of dreams* and hopes and problems, you will soon work out the real things in your life that may be frightening you, but which you cannot now admit to, or cope with.

Q: Can you be a dream major in college.

A: I'm told many colleges don't have majors anymore — it's said to be old fashioned. But perhaps you can specialize in psychology in college. Most of the people in the dream-research field started with some interest in psychology.

You can read books on the scientific and psychological aspects of dreaming. There are many different theories. You can learn to sort them out and develop your own point of view.

You might consider asking a favorite high school teacher where you could learn more about various aspects of dreaming. Perhaps you live near a university with a Sleep Laboratory. If so, you should visit the laboratory and talk to the many specialists there. Perhaps you can even work in this kind of laboratory on weekends during your senior year in high school.

Meanwhile you might want to ask your school and local librarian for dream material in journals and dream books. I think you will enjoy reading Ann Faraday's two books, *Dream Power* and *Dream Game*, and Patricia Garfield's *Creative Dreaming*. Then if you are very interested in the subject you can approach the more complicated works of Sigmund Freud, Alfred Adler, and Carl Jung.

Q: Do your dreams have anything to do with sleepwalking?

A: Sleepwalking occurs during other stages of sleep. During REM sleep stage when you are in deep sleep and in dreaming state, your body is entirely immobilized and cannot move.

Q: Is it so that if you have a dream three times it will come true?

A: It will not become true, but it does mean you are working out a very persistent problem. Put it down on paper with all the thoughts, feelings, sensations, places, and sounds that you can remember. Then try to find the objective meaning — the meaning that relates to your life. If you cannot find a literal meaning, Calvin Hall, the dream investigator, suggests looking at the dream as if it were a "distorted looking glass." Peer deeply into that looking glass and sift out the meaning of the dream. Don't impose any meaning on any dream ... let the dream speak out for itself.

If you can't understand the dream, put a question to your dream mind as I suggest elsewhere in the book. Ask the dream what it means; ask the dream to explain itself to you. If no answer is forthcoming, use the glass of water technique described on pages 59–60.

When I was young I *often* dreamed I was drowning in a swift stream that was carrying me away. I always pushed out a little straw for someone to catch. This dream always scared me, and I wondered about it. I wish now that I had had the sense to talk this dream over with my parents, and had made an opportunity of working out the problem(s) it reflected about my early childhood. I had been very sick and had almost died several times, and I had been hospitalized several times. I know that I had been very unhappy when I was left alone in those hospitals where they didn't allow my parents to visit me!

Another recurring dream I had for years, and many more than three times, I can assure you, was being in a fire and not being able to yell for help. I often tried practicing by shouting, "HELP," when I was alone, because I was afraid I would be unable to take care of myself in such an emergency.

I am sure these two dreams reflected deep feelings of anxiety and helplessness which I couldn't voice aloud.

Now you are living in a period of more freedom and considerably more understanding of the nature of these nightmares and dreams. That is why I think you should seriously consider sharing any such dreams (and good dreams too) with a *sympathetic* person in your family, or a dear friend you can trust.

It would be just great to start up a DREAM COMMUNITY where dreams are voiced aloud, and where the people (young and old) try to help each other to solve the wonderful mysteries dreams contain. Some teachers may want to help you explore this new world. But not all teachers would be interested in this project, so don't try to force the idea on any teacher, or leader of a group to which you belong.

If you cannot find anyone to start a dream community, you might put a note up on the school bulletin board for a meeting of a Dream Club. It might help to invite a pleasant and interested adult to sit in at this first meeting too, to help in getting the club started.

Also try keeping that dream journal on your own. Eventually you will meet others who are doing the same thing and will want to share their experiences.

Q: It seems pretty often I have dreams that I am falling downstairs head-first. Why is that?

A: Everyone falls sometimes, either in a dreamlet stage just before going off to sleep, or in the dreams themselves. Usually it is a sensation of falling through space.

Falling downstairs often must be a frightening experience. I imagine it actually happened to you when you were younger, and the fear of the experience keeps on occurring again and again. Perhaps it will just disappear when you get older.

Why not CONFRONT this nightmare type of dream?

Say to yourself just before going to sleep, "Dream, why are you frightening me? Dream, I don't want to fall downstairs anymore!"

Q: How is it that I can never remember faces in a dream when I wake up? Sometimes my best friend can be in a dream. You know it is your best friend, but you never even saw the face in the dream!

A: There are different roles in dreams. Sometimes there are active roles, other times people are passive. That is to say you just know certain people are there, but they are never really *in view*. Just as a photographer who is taking the picture can be seen by those in the photograph but is not in the picture, many dream presences are "known" but not visualized fully in the dream. As for actually identifying friends in dreams — trust your dream mind. It is *SMART*!

I have included the words PASSIVE and ACTIVE in the dream log so that you will be more aware of the roles you play in your dreams. The more control you have over your life, the more active a role you will play in your dreams.

Q: Is it true dreams only last for two seconds? If so, how come it seems as if they last a lot longer. One night I dreamed I was on a ship with my family and there was a shipwreck. I was the only survivor. It seemed real and lasted a couple of hours.

A: Some fragments of dreams may indeed last only two seconds or so, but dream experiences and recall vary from person to person. The longest type of dream lasts only twenty minutes, although many people experience a feeling of continuity from one dream period to another. Others have reported in letters to me that they dream continuous dreams from one night to another, that a football game that hasn't ended is continued at another time. All in all you dream two hours every night, and thus your long dream may have been a continuous one, as your mind unraveled this sense of being alone in the world or of wanting to be alone.

Q: Do you know a good way to have good dreams?

A: I've offered many suggestions in other parts of the book, but there is also an interesting mental imagery exercise that you can try.

Step one: Search your mind for a beautiful place that you have visited or seen in some movie or travel shot. Set this place in your mind. Let your eyes wander about the scene. Absorb the different colors of the sparkling river water, or ocean, or meadow with flowers, or beach front — whatever the scene is, *fix it in your mind*.

Step two: When you are sure you have the scene set, mentally walk around the scene to touch the plants or objects, to smell the sea air, or fragrant flowers, or pine woods.

Step three: After you have experimented with each of the above steps and have the beautiful place you want to revisit firmly implanted in your memory bank, you can start this experiment:

Count backwards in your mind: 10-9-8-7-6-5-4-3-2-1. Imagine you are DESCENDING in an elevator (or on an escalator) with each step. Keep envisioning yourself going down, down, down, until you hit the lowest level of stage one. Then count another 10-9-8 — down to 1 again, always going down, down, down in your mind.

When you reach the lowest stage you will be at the place you have chosen as a beautiful place you would like to revisit. Whatever the scene you have chosen, be it a cliff with an infinite view of other mountains and valleys, or a lagoon on the ocean where you can swim, a river bank with all kinds of remembered smells and sounds, a snow-studded mountain you would like to ski on, a trail through a woods, the majestic view of a Norwegian fjord, or the unforgettable view of Venice or the Taj Mahal — it's your scene. It can also be a fantasy place that you make up. What you should do, though, is try to stick to one particular spot so as not to confuse the exercise.

Walk around in your mind, touch the things in the scene, bathe in the water, ski down the slope, crunch through the autumn woods, depending on the scene you have chosen.

Breathe the air deeply. Enjoy the aroma of the setting. Look at the colors in your scene. Let yourself go and run around laughing and enjoying yourself as you did when you were a child, playing at your favorite make-believe. Breathe deeply so as to increase the gaiety and *calmness* and peace that will come over you.

Stay there ten minutes or so . . . or even longer if you like. It's your scene, your place, *and you can come back anytime you want to*.

To return, use the tools of psychology and take the elevator or escalator back up. 1-2-3-4-5-6-7-8-9-10 — Feel yourself slowly ASCENDING. Reach the first platform. Smile to yourself, and take the next elevator or escalator upwards. As you count, think of the calmness that has pervaded your body, and how very good you feel. Count 1-2-3-4-5-6-7-8-9-10. . . . Then count

1-2-3, snap your fingers, and return to real life *with a smile.*

You can use scenes like the one I propose or other imaginative scenes anytime you need a quick surge of energy, or a mental change of pace. This is an instant trip away in time and place and can help you to dream pleasant dreams.

If you should want to travel in space during the night (an easy task if you set your mind to it), you can count upwards 1-2-3-4-5-6-7-8-9-10, until you reach a platform on your escalator or elevator. Stop. Go up a mountainside on this machine of yours (you can even walk up — why not?). Count again: 1-2-3-4-5-6-7-8-9-10. You will have reached a cliffside or the highest part of a mountain in your strong leaps upward. You can be under the white clouds and feel as if you can almost touch the sky.

Now you can imagine that your body is free as a bird, and that you can fly on a bird, leap on a flying horse such as Pegasus, or any animal you may cherish, or that your own body can soar with the same joy and motion as a seagull.

This is how you really can set the mood for sleep, and how you can create imaginative and exciting experiences for your dream mind.

Q: When you have dreams, do you think them, visualize them, or is it something you think you dreamed?

A: All. You think and visualize these "pictures of the mind," and indeed sometimes you are even aware when you are dreaming that you *are* dreaming. That dream has a special name: Lucid Dream.

You can rearrange and change lucid dreams even more easily than other dreams. One ancient technique taught by some American Indians is to look at your hand during a dream. That will help you to remember that you are in a dream state, and will give you an opportunity to experiment within your dream and change and reconstruct the dream to be more positive for you.

Q: Do you have to be in a certain kind of mood to have a dream?

A: No matter what your mood is, you will dream. But the mood you are in is reflected as surely as would your image if you looked in a mirror.

Q: Many people dream of scary things, especially if scary things happened, or if there is a scary-type movie on TV. How does the mind remember all of these things?

A: The mind makes connections. You can also see a scary movie on TV that *doesn't* affect you at all. But when and if the scary situation relates to some unresolved childhood memory, or a recent personal problem that made you anxious, the TV can trigger a nightmare-type dream.

Many people, young and old, have learned that it is safer to avoid scary movies so that they can avoid a typical monster confrontation in their dream.

If you are prone to having scary dreams night after night, reread the section on nightmares and night terrors and daydreaming. You can learn to challenge and stop a nightmare, or a recurring monster visitor, or mean people, or angry animals.

You can train yourself to confront these difficult people, horrible objects, and bad situations by waking up from a nightmare and immediately redreaming the dream, with you as the winning challenger in the dream.

Q: Do blind people dream?

A: The age one becomes blind is usually a deciding factor. Ordinarily if one becomes blind before five years of age there are no visual images in dreams, but if blindness occurs after seven years of age the person can see details and images in dreams even after intervals of twenty to thirty years.

One exception to this seems to be Helen Keller. Helen Keller was only nineteen *months* old when she had an attack of scarlet fever that destroyed her sight, hearing, and sense of smell. This made her what we call deaf, dumb, and blind. However, as many of you may recall from that remarkable film *The Miracle Worker*, or through Helen Keller's own fascinating autobiography, *Story of My Life*, an outstanding woman, Anne Sullivan, came into her life when she was six years old. She changed Helen from a wild animal who could not function at all, into one of the great and most admirable scholars of our time.

Mark Twain met her and declared: "Along her special line Helen Keller is the most remarkable product of all ages." He persuaded an oil magnate, H. H. Rogers, to back Helen in a college education, and she went on to learn, through hand language and Braille, many foreign languages and most of the culture of her time.

This is what Helen Keller has said about dreaming.

My dreams do not seem to differ very much from the dreams of other people. Some of them are real and link to an event or conclusion; others have no meaning and are fantastic.

... I float wraithlike upon clouds, in and out amongst the winds, without the faintest notion that I am doing anything unusual.

... I visit a foreign land where I have not been in reality, and I converse with peoples whose language I have never heard. Yet we manage to understand one another perfectly.

I think I am more fortunate in my dreams than most people; for as I think back over my dreams, the pleasant ones seem to predominate, although we naturally recall most vividly and tell most eagerly the grotesque and fantastic adventures in Slumberland.

I like to think that in dreams we catch glimpses of a life larger than our own.

We see it as a little child, or as a savage who visits a civilized nation. Thoughts are imparted to us far above our ordinary thinking. Feelings nobler and wiser than any we have known thrill us between heartbeats. For one fleeting night a princelier nature captures us and we become as great as our aspirations.

Q: Do we all have to sleep the same amount of time?

A: Absolutely not. We are all constituted differently. We all need different amounts of food and vitamins, and some people need more sleep while others need less sleep. This seems to be genetic (inherited), and it also has something to do with the vitality and pleasure you find in life.

In general most people need about eight hours of sleep when they are adults. Children need more sleep, and then the need changes several times; thus it varies as you grow up and reach adulthood. And very old people need even less sleep.

While it is true that most people do not feel rested or relaxed unless they have what we think of as a full eight hours, there are some unusual people who just do not need much sleep. The inventor Thomas Edison was such a man. He slept only four hours each night and filled in the rest of the day with little catnaps on the floor of his laboratory (until his wife sent in a cot).

Edison once summed up his unusual ability to function in his diary: "Slept splendidly, evidentally inoculated with insomniac bacilli when a baby. Arose early, went out to flirt with the flowers."

Q: Do you have any favorite dream stories?

A: I do like this old one which I discovered in an American history journal:

It concerns the Englishman Sir William Johnson, who was appointed Superintendent of Indian Affairs in the young America. Being very rich and fastidious, he followed the fashions of the times and sent home to England for some richly textured and laced suits.

When they arrived, Hendrick, King of the Mohawk nation, was present and he admired them. A few days later Hendrick visited Sir William and told him he had had a dream. Sir William solicitously asked him to tell him the dream.

"I dreamed that you had given me one of

the fine suits that just arrived," Hendrick said.

Sir William took the hint from that dream and immediately bestowed one of the richest of the suits on the Indian chief. Hendrick was very pleased.

A few weeks later Sir William confided to Hendrick he too had had a dream, and Hendrick asked him to share it with him.

"I dreamed you made me a present of 5,000 acres of the best of the Mohawk Valley," Sir William replied solemnly.

Hendrick gave him a gift of the land immediately, and then said, "Now, Sir William, I will never dream with you again. You dream too hard for me."

Q: I've been trying to write down my dreams, but sometimes I cannot understand any of the stories or handwriting in the morning!

A: Cheer up! It happens to all of us, and since it is best to write in a sort of delayed trance state similar to sleep, so that you can retain the memories of the dream intact, you will frequently find your handwriting illegible. Have you tried using a tape recorder? Many serious dream readers do just that.

This reminds me of a story I heard of a well-known woman. She awakened with a feeling she had actually solved the riddle of the universe in a remarkable poem which she made sure to write down.

In the morning she recalled writing a poem and she couldn't wait to read it. She was pretty surprised to find:

> Hogamus Higamus
> Dogamus Digamus
> Higamus Hogamus
> Digamus Dogamus

Q: Dear sleep expert: I am going crazy. I can't seem to remember ANYTHING I study for exams. It's been terrible, and I am getting very nervous. I come home, take a nap, and then study long and hard. I have a pretty good memory, so why can't I remember anything, especially after having a good nap?

A: The clue is in the nap. Your timing is off it seems. Scientists at the University of Colorada have now discovered that possibly due to a sleep hormone which is very strong in the early stage of any sleep, that hardly *anyone* can remember things studied *after* a nap, or after being awakened from a deep sleep.

Dr. Eric Hoddes of the University of Colorado notes, in an article in *Psychology Today*, that while sleep helps us to remember, it is "only when sleep FOLLOWS study. If sleep comes just *before* study, it can turn out to be worse than no sleep at all."

This sleep hormone wears off as the night progresses; thus it is usually alright to study after a *complete* night's sleep, but Dr. Hoddes actually suggests allowing about four hours between sleep and important fact learning.

So you know at least that you are not alone in your problem. Take *no naps before cramming* for exams. If you are anxious about the exam, do some deep breathing to relax you, and stimulate your brain with a cold-water ankle splash, and a cold-water hand splash and face splash. Study, *then* take a nap. Eat supper, study again (keep some fresh air coming into the room), then sleep again. You'll find that this new pattern will help you to digest your school material. Let your dreaming and sleeping brain absorb the material.

Q: Since you are writing a book on dreaming, you must know sleep problems. Can you help me to find a sleep expert? I can hardly ever fall asleep.

A: There are many new ways of learning to fall asleep, but before I outline them, let me give you the name of a center. If your family physician cannot help you to find the answer to your problem, you can write to this center for the address of a clinic nearest to you: American Association of Sleep Disorders Centers, University of Cincinnati Sleep Disorder Center, Christian R. Holmes Hospital, Eden and Bethesda Avenues, Cincinnati, Ohio 45219.

I hope you will read this book thoroughly to more fully understand the nature of sleep and dreaming. You might be more willing to "let go," and give in to the delicious far-away feeling which we all have in the first stage of sleep.

Science has determined that this first stage is alpha. That is to say, they have given a name to the kind of brain wave we have in the first stage of sleep.

The Indians found a way to get to this state by meditation, and, in fact, many kinds of repeated prayers or chanting can help you to get to this serene moment of "passive blankness." The interesting thing about alpha waves is that you can actually *learn* to duplicate them. Yoga meditation and TM (transcendental meditation) both help you to find this state. You can also learn it by doing Dr. Herbert Benson's "Relaxation Response," by sitting calmly with your feet planted on the floor, hands relaxed, and repeating the number *one* over and over and over again.

Q: Do you have any suggestions for getting to sleep? It takes me a long, long time.

A: A wonderful method that I sometimes use when my mind won't let go and I seem to be thinking only of problems, is the *magic backward counting.*

Think of a blackboard, with an eraser and chalk.

Write the number 100 on the blackboard.

Pick up the eraser and erase it.

Write the number 99 on the board.

Pick up the eraser and erase it.

Write the number 98.

Keep on working backwards until you fall asleep. This really works! The concentration and the mental effort in writing and erasing the numbers should help you to fall asleep quickly. Most of the time people don't even go past 90, although sometimes people go way into the seventies. On one tough night I went to 56. But the idea is to see how *little* you can do before sleep overtakes you.

Q: Why do I seem to make a lot of mistakes the day after a night where I toss and turn all night? Is it because I am tired?

A: What an interesting question. You have zeroed in on some fascinating research done at the Veteran's Administration Hospital in Cincinnati, where Dr. Milton Kramer, Director of Research, has found out that one of the chief functions of sleep may be to regulate people's daytime moods.

While Dr. Kramer cautions us all that there may be other interpretations on the function of sleep, his research has indicated that the mood of each day may be connected to the *number* of people in one's dreams all night.

If you have had a lonely dream in which you are wandering alone in some deserted place, it may mean the next day will seem bleak and depressing. On the other hand, if you have a lot of people in your dreams, it is more than likely you will feel happy and "up" the next day.

"Being alone, even in your dreams, isn't much fun," explains Dr. Kramer.

Dr. Kramer sees a connection between the physical quality of sleep, and mistakes the next day. "You can usually attribute your poor performance to a poor night's sleep.